be a winner in
WINDSURFING

be a winner in
WINDSURFING

BY CHARLES COOMBS

illustrated with photographs and diagrams
William Morrow and Company
New York 1982

Printed in the United States of America.
1   2   3   4   5   6   7   8   9   10

Library of Congress Cataloging in Publication Data

Coombs, Charles Ira, 1914–
    Be a winner in windsurfing.
    Includes index.
    Summary: Describes windsurfing, also called boardsailing or sailboarding, and provides information about equipment, training, and techniques used in this relatively new sport. Includes a glossary of terms.
    1. Windsurfing—Juvenile literature. [1. Windsurfing] I. Title.
GV811.63.W56C66   797.1′72   82-2165
ISBN 0-688-01060-1   AACR2

Photo Credits

Permission for photographs is gratefully acknowledged: AMF Alcort, p. 91; Dufour Sailboards, p. 77; Funsurf, Inc., p. 122; Howmar Boats, Inc., p. 24; Kransco, p. 93; Sailrider, Inc., p. 29; Windsurfing International, Inc., pp. 4, 12, 19, 85, 95, 97 (photograph by Steve Wilkings), 99, 100, 115, 117, 120. All other photographs by the author.

Acknowledgment

Exploring any interesting subject leads a writer down diverse pathways or, in the case of this book, waterways. My investigation of windsurfing took me from the frigid straits along the west coast of Canada to the warmer climes of Southern California, where it all began more than a dozen years ago.

Wherever there was water, I usually located some gathering of boardsailors avidly pursuing their sport. Always they were cooperative and most willing to demonstrate their skills. Unfortunately, many were fleeting acquaintances, and I regret not being able to remember their names.

But a number of them I remember very clearly. June Everett and Kim Baldwin, for instance, invited me to their classes in which, after a few hours of instruction and simulator training, they converted hesitant beginners into confident and reasonably skilled windsurfers. Diana Gowman, Pat Study, and Kenny Thompson, three students who allowed me to focus my camera on them at all moments whether graceful or awkward, have all long since become experts.

At other teaching sessions and windsurfing events, instructors Gale Notestone, Eric Bonniot, and Bob Foote demonstrated the finer points of boardsailing. And there is no forgetting young Fred Gengenagel, who in a stiff breeze one day put his craft through a series of amazing freestyle stunts that showed what could be done with and on a sailboard.

Also I want to thank Ted Robbins, an instructor at Windsurfing West, in Marina del Rey, California, for checking out the manuscript for accuracy.

To these people and, of course, to all those others who provided both knowledge and illustrations, my heartfelt appreciation for allowing me to share their fun and for helping to make this book possible.

Charles "Chick" Coombs
Westlake Village, California
1982

contents

chapter one
WHAT WINDSURFING IS

Windsurfing—also called boardsailing or sailboarding—is a wind-and-water sport well suited to anyone seeking fun, adventure, and a challenge. It appeals particularly to those who like to test their skills, match wits, or simply enjoy a social day with friends at a lake or beach. Windsurfing can be a leisurely pastime or a fiercely competitive contest.

The windsurfer's craft consists of a small sail attached to an oversized surfboard. But, unlike a sailboat, it does not have stays, shrouds, and taut lines to support a firm mast and help control the sail. As a windsurfer, you depend entirely upon your own strength, coordination, and balancing skills to brace and manipulate a free-swinging mast and sail.

There are no standard physical requirements for becoming a windsurfer. You may be tall or short, fat or skinny, man or woman, boy or girl. You do need to be fit, however, in order to get the most out of the sport.

Sailborne, two-legged water bugs scoot across the rivers,
lakes, and oceans of the world.

Agility, strength, and coordination are all needed to
control a wind-whipped board scooting erratically over
ruffled water.

A relatively new sport, windsurfing is fast becoming
a popular pastime wherever there is wind and enough
water to float a boat, whether it is a pond, lake, river,
or an ocean. The initial equipment costs perhaps $600
to $1200, but expenses are minimal thereafter. You
don't need a boat trailer to transport a sailboard, nor
do you need to pay rent on a slip. A sailboard is
extremely light and portable. It fits onto any cartop

utility rack, tucks nicely into the back of a pickup truck, rides atop a van, or can be towed behind a bicycle. It can be assembled and put into the water within a few minutes of arrival at a sailing site. After a day's use, it is easily dismantled and toted home without the time-consuming cleanup and stowing away that other types of seacraft require. A sailboard also takes up little room and is easy to store.

Despite their close resemblance to surfboards, sailboards are recognized by the International Racing and Yachting Union (IRYU) as an official class of small watercraft. You can correctly refer to them as boats since they do have sails.

Today more than a million brightly colored windsurfing sails flutter across the waterways of the world, although no one can be sure just when or where

Windsurfing is a conveniently portable sport.

boardsailing originated. It is thought that prehistoric Amazonian Indians used crude hand-held sails made from jungle leaves to aid them in crossing rivers on hand-hewn planks shaped somewhat like crude surfboards. Other early people undoubtedly developed similar sail-borne methods for crossing water barriers. Yet there is little documentary proof.

The modern type of windsurf sailing, however, seems to have started twenty or thirty years ago when a few people began to experiment with combining a sail and a surfboard. Still, no one apparently bothered to pursue the idea professionally or to keep a record of important activities.

The first serious development of this new water sport is credited to two young Southern Californians, one an avid small-boat sailor named James Drake and the other a surfing enthusiast named Hoyle Schweitzer. They met at a beach party in the mid 1960s and were drawn to each other by a common interest in sailing and surfing. Soon they were discussing and sketching ways in which the two activities might be combined.

They encountered immediate problems. A flat, narrow surfboard is inherently unstable in the water. Having neither keel to steady it nor rudder to guide it, it bobs lightly atop the surface. A surfer can lie prone

14

A sailboard is skittish, so count on some falls.

on the board without upsetting it due to the low center of gravity. But he or she needs additional balance in order to kneel and paddle the board without tipping over. Only an extremely skillful surfer can stand upright on most normal-sized surfboards. The peak of surfing is reached when the surfer can stay on his or her feet and ride the curl of a wave shoreward. A surfboard, at best, is like a skittish colt determined to throw its rider.

And now Schweitzer and Drake began planning to add a sail to the unstable shallow-draft board, which would further upset its balance. Drake first tried using a simple, hand-held sail that resembled a large, string-

15

less kite. It didn't work. The slightest cross breeze tipped him over or pulled him off the small craft. Drake and Schweitzer discarded the idea. There had to be some better way to anchor and control the sail.

Why not convert the board into a small sailboat? Just stick a mast into the center of the board, and attach a small sail to it. This idea didn't work, either. Lacking a keel, the board toppled over when the slightest gust of wind hit the sail. Besides, there was no room for shrouds, stays, or booms with which to anchor and control the sail.

Schweitzer and Drake concluded that the sail had to be mounted flexibly so that the sailor could move it quickly in any direction needed to adjust to the constantly changing wind and water. Only by subtle movements of a flexible sail, aided by skillful body balance, could a windsurfer hope to escape repeated duckings.

To acquire that flexibility, Drake and Schweitzer developed a freely rotating socket located at the foot of a lightweight mast. It worked like a universal joint, able to swing, bend, or pivot in any direction, and became the key to what is now called a "free-sail system." Since there were no rigging ropes or wires to support the mast, the sailor had to do so instead. He or

16

The flexible mast foot is the key to boardsailing.

she stood beside the mast, took hold of a specially designed boom, and twisted or inclined the sail in any way needed in order to catch and control the constantly changing wind. This type of delicate and pliable control was what enabled the sailor to propel and steer the board without tipping over.

The second important development was a wishbone-shaped boom with which the sailor can control the movement of the sail. The boom, actually a pair of connected booms, bends around the mast and stretches along both sides of the sail. The fore and aft ends are held securely together by special connectors. The forward connector often includes a convenient handle and a soft rubber bumper to protect the hull in case mast and boom crash onto it. The forward end of the boom attaches to the mast, while the aft end serves as

17

The sailboard is controlled with hand-held booms.

the anchor spot for the outer tip, or clew, of the basically triangular sail.

Regardless of which side of the sail the sailor is on, one or the other of the paired booms provides a handhold for controlling the movement of the sail.

After much trial and error, Schweitzer and Drake produced a sailboard on which they were able to stand upright and steer by a combination of deft movements of the sail and careful body balance. In 1969, they

18

From Boston to Bruges, boardsailors skim across
the waterways of the world.

patented the newly designed sailboard under the trade name of Windsurfer.

The word *windsurfing*, which seemed aptly descriptive, developed from the trade name and quickly became the most popular term for the exciting new water sport.

However, the new sport did not gain popularity as quickly in the United States as it did in Europe, where so many people seemed to be located conveniently near some body of navigable water. Also, the Europeans were especially receptive to a challenging yet inexpensive summer substitute for winter skiing.

Several European manufacturers were licensed to produce Windsurfer sailboards, and others quickly developed their own designs. In France, Germany, Holland, Sweden, and Italy, the sport gained immediate popularity, and the name of boardsailing came into currency for the activity. Soon it was taken up in virtually every part of the world. Windsurfers skimming across the Nile River, jumping the waves off Tahiti, or cavorting on the ruffled waters of Lake Titicaca high in the Peruvian Andes became a common sight.

Indeed, windsurfing has become the fastest growing and most popular water sport of the 1980s.

chapter two

THE SAILBOARD SYSTEM

Dozens of different makes and styles of sailboards are now being manufactured throughout the world. There are big ones, small ones, hard and soft ones. There are plain white boards and boards of many colors. Some are designed primarily for stability and are well suited for general recreational sailing on fairly smooth water in moderate wind. Other smaller, lightweight, stream-lined boards are more sensitive, demand more skill in handling, and are preferred for racing, surf riding, wave jumping, and other high-performance activities.

However, all sailboards are considered a free-sail system and are composed of two major parts—the hull (board) and the rig (sail).

Many different combinations of fiberglass and plastics are used in sailboards. A few boards are hollow; a few are made of polyethelene foam. By far the most prevalent, however, are hulls that have an outside shell of hard polyethelene plastic packed with a tightly

Hull and flexibly mounted rigging
make up the free-sail system.

beaded polyurethane foam core that provides additional strength and is amply buoyant. All windsurfing boats are nonsinkable.

A hull that is used in quiet water may be quite flat. But since the real fun of windsurfing is to challenge both wind and waves, most boards are bent upward, or scooped, several inches at the bow. This design helps the board skim over rough water and largely prevents pearling, or nosediving under the water. The stern of the board may also be bent upward slightly, or rockered, to aid in steering.

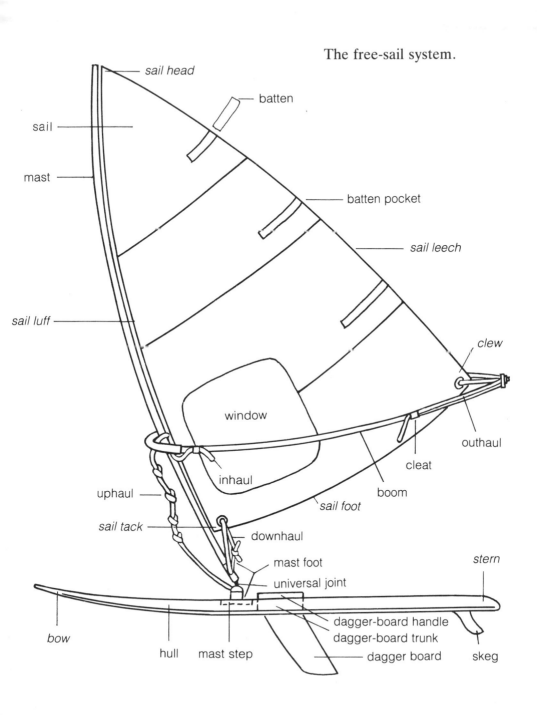

The free-sail system.

sail head

batten

sail

mast

batten pocket

sail leech

sail luff

clew

window

inhaul

outhaul

uphaul

cleat

boom

sail tack

sail foot

downhaul

stern

mast foot

universal joint

bow

dagger-board handle

dagger-board trunk

hull

mast step

dagger board

skeg

Lightweight, narrow, slightly V-bottomed hulls are faster than flattish hulls. They also are more demanding, and a windsurfer must be particularly skillful in order to get the best performance out of them. The lighter hull floats higher out of the water, so there is less water friction on it. Thus, it has greater speed, although less stability, and is preferred for racing. On the other hand, the longer and wider the board, the more stable it is in the water. With a heavy sailor aboard, it sinks still deeper and is slowed further by the greater water friction.

A lightweight board is used
for high-performance action.

So you should decide on the size, shape, and weight of your board according to the use you intend to make of it. Generally, a good sailboard for recreational windsurfing is one with a medium-weight hull weighing about 40 pounds (18 kilograms) that is approximately 12 feet long (about 3½ meters) and 2 feet (⅔ of a meter) wide, scooped and rockered slightly fore and aft. With such a board, you can handle most water and wind conditions nicely.

After you choose your first one, you can move in any direction you wish by selling, trading, buying, or borrowing the hull that best suits your purposes. Like a skier or sailboater, you probably will find yourself trying out, bartering, and constantly upgrading your equipment according to whether your current preference is for simple recreational activity, high-speed racing, or the fancy tricks of freestyle windsurfing.

There is more to a hull, however, than just the board. Unlike an ordinary surfboard, a sailboard needs a dagger board. Thrust down into the water in the same manner as the centerboard of a small sailing boat, the dagger board provides lateral resistance. It helps prevent the hull from skidding sideways in the water when a quartering or side wind pushes against the sail. It adds the stability of a small keel and enables the craft to sail into the wind. However, a dagger board adds a considerable amount of drag to the hull. Hence, dagger boards are manufactured in different sizes and shapes to fit various needs. A racing dagger board, for example, is smaller than one used for normal cruising.

Most dagger boards are engineered and especially notched so you can withdraw them partially or all the way up out of the dagger-board trunk, an oblong, reinforced slot sliced through the hull near its center. This adjustment can be made with a nudge of your foot or by pulling the dagger board up by its handle while the sailboard is under way. The dagger board must fit securely into its slot, yet not so tightly that you cannot insert, adjust, or withdraw it readily when the need arises.

The dagger board serves as a removable keel,
giving lateral stability to the sailboard.

In shallow water, a dagger board can hit a reef or drag on the beach and cause considerable damage. You must be aware of this danger and pull it up in plenty of time. But if your dagger board is made of pliable material that will give under pressure, it will be more durable. Yet it must be stiff enough to remain firm when moving sideways through the water. Most are made of wood, plastic, or a hard, rubberized compound.

Near the aft end of the hull is a skeg. Sometimes a sailboard has two or even three of them. The skeg is a small, stationary fin set beneath the stern. Not really a rudder, for it does not move, the skeg keeps the sailboard aimed straight ahead and prevents it from fishtailing. It is similar to those used on ordinary surfboards, but larger. A sailboard skeg is usually

A skeg keeps the sailboard aimed straight ahead; the dagger board provides stability to the hull.

somewhere between six and twelve inches long and shaped like a downthrusting shark's fin.

Different-sized skegs may be used according to wind and water conditions. Ideally, you should be able to remove a skeg and replace it with a smaller or larger one as you wish. The skeg works in combination with the dagger board, but usually the stronger the wind, the larger the skeg needed to provide stability. Thus, skegs are usually screw-mounted to simplify removal or changing.

Some hulls have mounting places for several skegs. The need for more than one is determined by how you intend to use your board and how much forward stability you want. Generally, the skeg that comes on the board is sufficient for recreational use. In fact, often it is permanently fastened in place.

In addition to the dagger-board trunk, there is a second reinforced hole cut into the center of the sailboard hull. It is the mast step, into which the mast foot slips. It might be rectangular or round, depending on the shape of the mast foot. The sailboard may have one or more sockets, so you can choose the mast position that is best for the wind conditions and your weight. Like the hull, the mast foot comes in many different styles.

Thus, with the hull properly designed and built for stability and strength, slotted for a dagger board, equipped with a skeg, and provided with some kind of mast step, it is ready to be rigged.

The sailboard's rig is made up of three main parts—the mast, the sail, and the boom. Actually, these parts form the power source, or "motor," of any sailing craft. But there are significant differences in the mast, sail, and boom of a sailboard.

More than anything else, the loosely hinged, universal-jointed mast separates a sailboard from all other sailing vessels. It is the one thing that enables you to steer a sailboard or, indeed, to stay upright on it.

Mast, sail, and wishbone boom
form a sailboard's "motor."

The sailboard mast is approximately 14 feet (about 4 meters) tall. It is generally made of polyester, fiberglass, aluminum alloy, or even more expensive graphite compounds. Usually hollow, the mast tapers gradually toward the upper tip and is reinforced near the base where it takes heavy strain. It must be flexible in order to bow slightly under a taut sail and also to absorb the shock of gusting winds. Yet it must be strong enough to withstand the force of the wind and the battering it may get from time to time when it topples into the water. At the top, it is plugged so it will not fill with water.

The mast foot is designed to fit firmly into the mast step, although usually it should not lock into place. There are times, particularly during a spill, when the mast foot should pop out from the step to prevent wrenching or cracking the hull or pinching an arm or foot painfully between the mast and the board. On the other hand, it should fit tightly enough into the step so that it will not come out accidentally in high winds or rough water. A mast foot with a mechanical locking device that holds it into the step until you flip the release is helpful.

The important universal joint itself may be made up of a ball-and-socket coupling not unlike that used on

The sailboard mast is inserted into a special socket
in the hull.

an automobile drive shaft. Or it may be a heavy but
flexible solid rubber joint that bends easily in any
direction yet connects mast and board firmly together.
The main requirement is that the universal allows the
mast to tilt and rotate freely.

The second component of a sailboard's rig is the sail
itself. Sails come in many sizes, shapes, and colors.
Most are made of wrinkle-resistant Dacron, similar to
that of quality sails on other small sailing craft.
Sometimes Mylar or other strong, lightweight, water-
shedding types of synthetic-fiber sailcloths are used.

All sails are carefully designed to make the best use of the wind and are assembled panel by panel in a sail loft. Although plain white sailcloth is preferred by a few and is thought to be more durable and resistant to stretch, most windsurfers (as do most hang gliders and hot-air balloonists) strongly favor the bright colors. So you will see veritable rainbows of reds, blues, greens, and yellows in all shadings and combinations wherever windsurfers gather.

While maneuvering over the water, you must constantly remain alert to everything going on around you. Since a solid sail certainly would block your vision much of the time, all windsurfing sails have one or more windows set into them so you can see what is happening on the other side of your sailboard. The windows are made of transparent plastic and are designed to be an integral part of the sail. They are also pliable enough to be rolled or folded with the sail.

Sails come in many sizes. Large ones are for light air and calm water conditions. Smaller storm sails are for high winds and rough seas. You quickly learn to use no more sail than you can control under any particular conditions. An average size is about 56 square feet (about 5 square meters) of fabric. A strong person in a modest breeze may carry an extra 6 feet (almost 2 meters) of sail without any problem. But a racer in a high wind may cut back to a storm sail of 45 square feet (approximately 4 square meters) or less. Some dedicated windsurfers carry a whole selection of sails in order to be prepared for any situation.

A sleeve, or socket, is sewed onto the forward, or luff, edge of the sail. This sleeve, often made of a sturdier material than the sailcloth itself, simply slips over the length of mast. Thus, the need to lash the sail to the mast is neatly taken care of. A notch, or open slot, is cut in the sleeve about a third of the way up the mast where the boom is attached.

As in the case of most boat sails, batten pockets are sewed into the trailing, or leech, edge of the sail. Stiffening battens, usually narrow plastic slats, are

Battens inserted into pockets sewn along the leech
help shape the sail.

inserted into the pockets to help keep the sail properly shaped to catch the wind.

The final major component of the rig is the boom. It serves to stretch out the sail and provides you with a device for steering the board. Shaped somewhat like a wishbone, although meeting at both ends, the boom curves along each side of the sail, enclosing it within its two arms. Thus, no matter which side of the sail you find yourself on, you can control the sailboard. Usually friction cleats are mounted near the fore and aft ends of the boom. They are used to snug down inhaul and outhaul lines.

Early windsurfing booms were made of teak or mahogany, and some are still around. But the common material now is largely aluminum tubing, which is both lighter and stronger. Usually the boom is wrapped with tape, or a bicycle inner tube is slipped over it to provide a nonslip grip.

Such are the basic parts of a sailboard. Your ability as a windsurfer depends upon how you put them together and what you are able to do with them afterward.

chapter three

PREPARING TO SAIL

When boardsailing, you are in direct contact with the wind and water. Thus, except in tropical climes, you may often be exposed to unusual amounts of cold. In moderate amounts, the cold generated by both wind and water causes little discomfort, and you may be content to do your windsurfing in swimming shorts or bathing suit. On the other hand, prolonged exposure to water of 70 degrees Fahrenheit (approximately 21 degrees Celsius) or below is hazardous. If not controlled, it can even be fatal as hypothermia can occur.

Hypothermia develops whenever the surrounding cold drains the heat from your body faster than you can regenerate it. Early warnings of hypothermia are shivering, faster breathing, and a lessening of strength and muscular dexterity—any or all of which you may be tempted to ignore in the excitement of windsurfing action.

In the summer, you may need more protection from

the sun than cold, but probably you will stretch your windsurfing season for as long as possible into the fall or even winter. Shorts, swimming trunks, a bathing suit, or a T-shirt and a pair of jeans may be fine for summer windsurfing, but when the season changes and both air and water grow colder, you need additional insulation.

A wet suit of some kind is the best protection from excessive exposure to cold water and a chilling wind. The most popular windsurfing wet suits are made of 1/8-inch (3-millimeter) thick neoprene, a synthetic rubber material foamed with tiny bubbles for insulation and lightness. The suit usually is inner lined with nylon for added strength and ease in dressing. The wet suit's exterior also may be partly or totally covered with nylon to strengthen it further and to brighten the black neoprene with a touch of color. However, nylon does not shed water as readily as a slick neoprene surface does, so many prefer to do without the bright coloring of an outer covering.

The function of a wet suit is to trap a thin film of water between your body and the suit. This water is kept warm by your body temperature and is held in place by the fitted suit, thus affording the needed insulation.

Cold water conditions call for wet-suit protection.

At times, a full wet suit that covers body, arms, and legs generates more heat than is necessary or even wanted. However, there are different styles. Some come in separate pieces so you can put on or take off as much as wind and water dictate. You can get basic long johns, which are similar to a farmer's overalls. The long johns leave your arms and shoulders free for action. If your upper body becomes chilled, you can add a jacket with either short or long sleeves. Or you may find that a short suit that insulates your torso but leaves your arms and legs free provides ample warmth.

Just about anything you need—long pants, short pants, vests, neoprene boots, socks—is available. So you can assemble your outfit according to the environment in which you will be doing your windsurfing. You will need more protection for cold winds and frigid water, less for mild conditions. Don't overbuy, for you can always add pieces as the need arises. Always look for quality if you want your suit to last. Check the seams for tightness and the inner lining for smoothness. If you will be doing any saltwater windsurfing, shun metal zippers. Salt water will corrode them until they no longer operate. Plastic zippers are generally used on the better suits. Just be sure there are enough, particularly around the wrists and ankles, so that you can get in or out of your suit without being a contortionist.

The suit, or any of its components, must fit snugly but not too tightly. There should be enough flexibility around shoulders, elbows, and knees to enable full freedom of movement.

The top of most boards is roughened up a little during manufacture so your feet will not slip on the wet deck. If it is not, you can do your own roughing, but

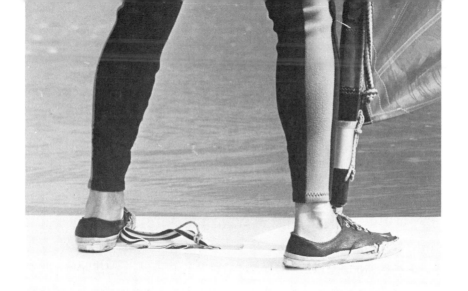

Almost any soft-soled shoes, new or old,
aid traction on the board.

carefully, with a file or coarse sandpaper. If you find
your bare feet won't stick properly to the board, you
can improve traction by wearing a pair of soft-soled
boat shoes, thin-soled running shoes, or canvas gym
shoes. Canvas does not provide much warmth, so you
might wear a pair of socks under them also. Not only
do shoes provide traction on the board, they protect
your feet from underwater hazards such as rocks, sharp
coral, broken glass, or other beach clutter.

Gloves will help improve your grip on the boom, but
they are bulky and lessen the sensitivity needed in your
fingers to adjust the boom to every slight pressure from
wind or wave. Gloves are worn more in high-wind,

cold-weather competition than during normal recreational sailboarding.

On hot sunny days, a T-shirt, a cap or visor, and sunscreen lotion are helpful protection against sunburn or even sunstroke. Then, if you don't overdo the exposure, you should stay comfortable and develop a tan instead of trouble.

Now prepared with board and sail, and properly dressed for the occasion, you are anxious to rig your boat and head for the water. But wait, windsurfing is not all that simple. Before going off on your own, you would be wise to sign up for a couple of lessons. They are available, either free or at low cost, wherever windsurfing is taking place.

Windsurfing students get a presail briefing.

In any case, you should familiarize yourself with a sailboard and learn the names of its parts. Before trying to rig your own boat, you should watch and listen to an experienced windsurfer, preferably a certified instructor. He or she will point out each part, explain what it does, and demonstrate how to assemble and use it.

After a general briefing on what windsurfing is about and the manner in which wind and water work upon a sailboard, the instructor may have you step onto a dry land simulator. The typical simulator is simply a chopped-down center section of a sailboard mounted on a freely rotating stand.

On the simulator, under the watchful eye of the instructor, you quickly learn the basics of raising the sail, positioning your hands on the boom, and placing your feet properly on the board. Soon you will be able to deal with the gentle gusts of wind without having taken the inevitable duckings you would in the water. Fifteen minutes or so on the simulator builds early confidence and gives you a feel of the free-sail system.

Following your equipment briefing and simulator time, you are more anxious than ever to try out a real sailboard on real water. So, as your instructor watches, you start to rig your sail. At the moment, you don't need the hull, so you leave it lying off to one side.

The simulator is an excellent teaching aid.

Until now, the sail has been folded up or wrapped around the mast. Or it may have been neatly stored in a separate sail bag, along with the battens. The assembled boom is not yet attached to either the mast or sail.

As you lay out the colorful Dacron or Mylar, try to remember how your instructor did so. For your own benefit, quietly rehearse a few important terms you have become acquainted with. For instance, there are three sides to a triangular sail. The forward edge of the sail is the luff, the edge is the leech, and the bottom of the sail is the foot. There is also the tack, which is the lower front corner of the sail; the clew, which is the rearward, or aft, corner of the sail, and the head, which is the corner at the top of the mast.

Now, while the mast is lying flat on the beach, you plug the upper end to keep it watertight. Then you slip the mast up into the long sock, or sleeve, sewed along the luff edge of the sail. Taking the short mast foot with the universal joint attached, shove it solidly up into the mast. If your sail uses battens, slide them into their pockets along the leech of the sail.

Get the wishbone boom assembly and place it around the mast so there is a boom on each side of the sailcloth. The protective bumper, or handle, at the front of the connecting booms rests at the cutaway slot in the mast sleeve. Be sure the boom is right side up so the line by which you will later hoist the mast and sail out of the water emerges downward from the bumper.

Using the inhaul line, you lash the boom tip to the mast. You can use any of several knots, as long as it will not slip and can be easily untied whether wet or dry. A bowline works nicely. In fact, you should

TOP: Lash the boom to the mast with the inhaul line.
BOTTOM: Four important nautical knots.

Use the reef knot to tie line ends together.

A clove hitch for attaching a line to the mast or spar shares many uses with the bowline.

Two half hitches will secure a line to any stationary part.

A bowline knot is suitable for securing the inhaul, outhaul, and downhaul lines.

become adept at tying it since it is one of any sailor's most effective knots. A clove hitch or a rolling hitch (which is simply a clove hitch with an extra loop to it) can also be used.

Be sure the boom is tied securely to the mast so it cannot slip up or down while you are sailing. If you are short, tie the boom low on the opening in the mast sleeve; if tall, move it up a little. You'll quickly find the most comfortable position.

With the boom in place and the extra line tied off with a couple of half hitches or snapped into a cleat often provided for that purpose, swing the boom out at a right angle to the mast so the connected aft ends lie out near the clew. Now, using the outhaul line slipped through the metal eye in the clew, stretch the sail out toward the aft end of the boom. Pull it fairly tight. However, it should not be pulled so flat that wind pressure won't bulge it out properly and give it the essential airfoil shape. You may want to adjust it later. A bowline knot works nicely here also. Tie off or cleat down any extra line. Use a nonslipping reef knot, or square knot, wherever you need to tie two lines together or repair a broken line.

Go forward now and pull the sail taut on the mast. Run a short new line, the downhaul, through the metal

The outhaul stretches the sail clew
toward the outer end of the boom.

grommet in the sail tack and secure it to the mast base.

Thus, three lines—inhaul, outhaul, and downhaul—
secure the boom to the mast and stretch the sail down
and out to catch the wind.

The time has come now to make a final check. Knots
all secure? Mast plugged? Battens, if any, in place?
Sail taut but not pulled too flat? Is your wet suit
zipped? Shoes not filled with sand? Are you going to
sail in an area where life jackets are mandatory? If so,
have one on. You are almost ready to raise the sail and
head for deep water—almost. But don't rush it.

chapter four
SAFE SAILING

Before you launch your boat and attempt to sail, you should first learn a few important facts about both wind and water. These forces can help you or threaten you, depending upon how well or poorly you use them.

Without wind, you have no fuel for your sail. Too much wind is more fuel than you can handle. It is essential that you always know from which direction the wind is blowing. Without this knowledge, you cannot set a sail or lay a course. Also, careful attention to wind direction enables you to avoid dangerous situations—such as unwittingly being blown out to sea.

There are several ways to read the path of the wind. Surface waves are usually generated by the wind and move in the same direction it does. You can also check wind direction by watching how it wafts smoke from a chimney or flutters the telltale ribbons or flags on boats anchored nearby. You can toss a bit of sand or a few dry leaves into the air and see which way they drift to earth; or you can always resort to holding up a wet finger and noting which side the wind chills.

A wind can strike from any point of the compass, but generally it is classified as onshore, blowing from water to land; offshore, blowing from land to water; or parallel, blowing along the beach or shoreline from either direction.

Of course, you also are concerned with the strength of the wind. You cannot windsurf in a calm, and you would be foolish to venture out in a raging gale. But there are a number of wind strengths in between these extremes. Many windsurfers judge velocities according to the Beaufort scale. Established by British Admiral Sir Francis Beaufort in 1805, this table for measuring wind forces at sea remains a worldwide standard.

The Beaufort scale starts at Force 0, which goes from dead calm to air moving at one knot, or a little more than one mile, per hour. At the far end of the scale is Force 12, which takes in hurricane winds of over sixty-five knots, or approximately seventy-five miles per hour.

As an average recreational windsurfer, you are most interested in wind conditions from Force 1 (breezes of from one to three knots that generate small ripples on the water) through Force 5 (fresh winds of between seventeen and twenty-one knots that kick up some

Beaufort Number	Wind speed (Knots)	Wind Description	Sea Condition
0	less than 1	calm	glassy
1	1–3	light air	rippled
2	4–6	light breeze	small wavelets
3	7–10	gentle breeze	wavelets with slight cresting
4	11–16	moderate breeze	small waves, some whitecaps
5	17–21	fresh breeze	moderate waves, more whitecaps
6	22–27	strong breeze	large waves, foamy crests
7	28–33	near gale	breaking sea heaps, streaks of foam
8	34–40	gale	moderately high waves and spindrift
9	41–48	strong gale	high waves, cresting and breaking with spray and foam
10	49–55	storm	very high, tumbling waves
11	56–65	violent storm	exceptionally high waves, spray and poor visibility; most
12	over 65	hurricane	dangerous of white-water seas

The Beaufort scale of sea-wind velocities.

spray and build up medium-sized whitecapped waves). Forces 2, 3, and 4 (winds varying from four to eighteen knots and water steadily showing more activity) are ideal for the windsurfer with average to expert skill. Forces 6, 7, and 8 winds (twenty-two to forty knots) are for daredevils only. Beyond that, regardless of how daring—or foolish—you may be, stay on the beach!

While boardsailing you will seldom be able to rely for any length of time on a steady breeze. The wind is forever puffing, swirling, changing direction, and otherwise threatening to upset your sailboard. So learn to read the signs. Gathering clouds on the horizon usually mean the approach of a storm front. Beware that you don't venture out so far that you get caught in it. Dark cat's-paws, or patches of riffles moving faster and at odds with the normal waves, indicate surging gusts of wind spinning in from various angles. You needn't try to avoid these minor maelstroms. Just be prepared to trim sail and adjust your balance in order to ride through them.

Actually, you are dealing with a combination of two winds. The first is the true wind, which is the one you feel when you are standing still. The second is the wind that is generated by motion, like the wind you feel on your face as you ride a bicycle on a calm day. When you combine the true wind with the motion-generated wind, you get what is known as the apparent wind. Although you may not be aware of it, you sail your boat according to the apparent wind, for it is the one that really affects your course and determines how much you must trim your sail.

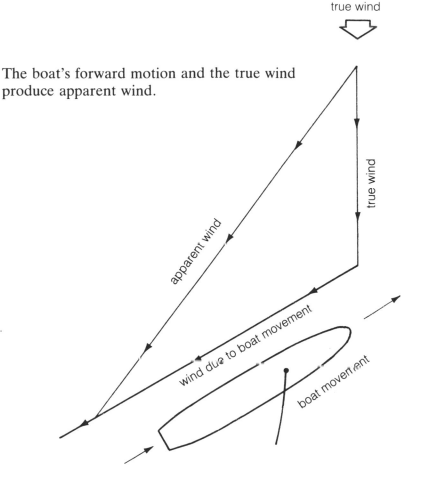

true wind

The boat's forward motion and the true wind produce apparent wind.

true wind

apparent wind

wind due to boat movement

boat movement

Because there is no motion-generated wind when running ahead of a true wind, there is no way you can make your craft go faster than the wind itself. In fact, due to the friction of the water dragging on the hull, you must go considerably slower than the true wind. But when the craft is sailing at an angle to the wind, there is both a true wind and a motion-generated wind. Then you may be able to work your sail to use this combined, or apparent, wind and increase your speed. Sand sailors and ice boaters are well acquainted with the possibilities for squeezing extra speed from the apparent wind.

Learn all you can about the wind and how it acts upon your sail. Realize that your sail is similar to an airplane's wing except that a sail operates in a vertical position and a wing operates in a horizontal position. For the sail, the lift is forward instead of upward. The curvature of the sail splits the air through which it passes just as the curvature of a wing does. The air travels more slowly along the near, or windward, side of the sail than it does on the longer, outer arc of the leeward curve. The slower air causes a pressure on the windward side of the sail, while the faster-moving air on the lee side generates a slight vacuum. The difference in pressures causes the sail to move toward the

The wind blowing across the sail produces
an aerodynamic force that moves the boat forward.

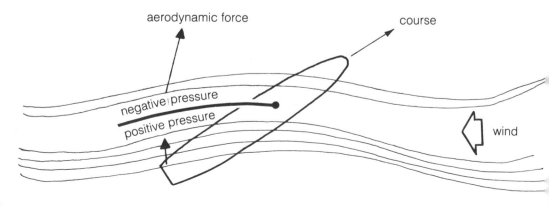

vacuum, or forward. This motion carries the hull, and you, with it.

The entire secret of successfully operating any sail craft in an upwind direction is to be able to trim, or sheet in, the sail at the precise angle that gives it a proper airfoil shape and produces maximum forward thrust. If you do not trim in enough, the wind fails to harden the sail. It simply flutters, or luffs. Without power, the board wallows and goes nowhere. If you sheet in too much, you also spoil the sail's airfoil pattern. The airflow starts to break down, or form burbles, on the leeward side. The sail stalls and generates less power. The direct force of the wind on the sail heels the board over on its side and may well catapult you into the water.

So no matter in which direction you want to go, you must learn to trim your sail to just the right degree of angle to the wind in order to produce the greatest amount of forward thrust while still maintaining control over its force. Success usually depends upon how diligently you practice.

In addition to knowing your winds, you must pay strict heed to water conditions. Water that has swift-running tides, is overly rough, or is full of swirling currents is generally poor for windsurfing. Water that is frigid, obstructed by protruding rocks, or sprinkled with shallows that can rip the dagger board or skeg from your hull should also be avoided. Even if you want to challenge some of these hazards, you would be wise to study the water conditions, ask questions of those familiar with the area, and check things out carefully before launching your board.

Meanwhile, remember that your sailboard is not a mere toy. Officially it is a class of boat, just like a Sabot, Cyclone, Laser, Hobie Cat, and many more luxurious sailing craft. Therefore, as a windsurfer, whenever you are on charted waters or sailing in any kind of traffic, you must be aware of and abide by the nautical rules of the road. These rules use the terms *port* and *starboard* for the words *left* and *right.* As you face the front, or bow, of a boat, everything on the left is to port, or on the port side, and everything on the right is to starboard, or on the starboard side.

The United States Coast Guard requests that you pay attention to warning buoys and navigational markers just like any other sailor. You must also keep to the starboard when approaching another craft head on. When taking any action, do so soon enough to make your intention clear to other boats.

Stay clear of swimmers, harbor entrances, and commercial shipping channels. And don't be too rigid

WINDSURFING
REGULATIONS

WINDSURFING
LAUNCHING AREAS

LAUNCHING AND/OR USE
NOT PERMITTED ON
WEEKENDS AND HOLIDAYS
9:00 A.M. TO 6:00 P.M.
EXCEPT AT SMALL BOAT SAILING LAGOON.
WEST END BASIN "D"
CO. ORD. 9359 SEC. 411
ALL BOATING REGULATIONS
MUST BE OBSERVED
FOR FURTHER INFORMATION
CONTACT HARBOR PATROL
TELEPHONE 820 1571

Windsurfers must abide by local rules
and Coast Guard regulations.

about what rights you think you have. If you insist that
being on a starboard tack gives you the right-of-way
over a boat on port tack, be sure that the boat is no
bigger than yours. If you happen to glance back and
see a steel bow towering over your stern, you might as
well veer off.

As a matter of fact, you would be wise to forget the
old sail-over-steam rule. Not only are you too small
and vulnerable to challenge a tugboat or a cruiser; the

By exercising safety precautions
and abiding by the nautical rules of the road,
boardsailors can share most waters
with other vessels, large and small.

rule itself is shot through with exceptions. A deep-sea vessel in a narrow channel certainly is not going to give way to a sailboard, nor is she required to. Fishing boats going about their business need not clear out of your way. And never try to uphold your right-of-way over any kind of naval vessel.

The only rule to follow is the one that says don't be foolish. Sail defensively. Your sailboard is not only the smallest and most fragile boat on the water, it is the most maneuverable. You can make it go forward, sideways, or backward. Make good use of that agility. Simply stay clear of any potentially dangerous situation, and you will enjoy your windsurfing for many years to come.

56

chapter five
GETTING LAUNCHED

Windsurfing can be extremely strenuous. You must use most of your muscles as you push, pull, and twist in order to convert the force of the wind in the sail to propulsion power in the board. Your body and limbs form that all-important connecting link through which you transfer this energy. To handle the task, you must stay in shape. You cannot afford to have a muscle tie up or pull a ligament just when you are straining to sheet in the sail against a stiff wind.

So, before you launch your sailboard, allow yourself a little time to loosen up. Do what any athlete does before a contest. Exercise with some sit-ups and torso twists to tone up your stomach muscles. Try a few squats for your legs and thighs. Or lie on your back and pedal an imaginary bicycle. Push-ups, or perhaps some less strenuous exercise, will shape up your arms and shoulders. Then shake them out to loosen up. Do whatever you can to strengthen your hand grip. The preparation will pay off later when you are grasping the boom with aching fingers.

Now get ready to launch your boat. Some windsurfers put sail and hull together on land, then drag the assembly to the water. Generally, however, the easier and more convenient way is to do the work in the water.

For the moment, leave your board ashore and take the rigging to the water first. If the wind is onshore, carry the rig out flat over your head with the mast sideways in front of you in both hands and the boom pointed into the wind. If the wind is offshore, at your back, you may need to change the position of the boom in order to keep it pointed into the wind. In either case, you must try to keep the wind out of the sail, or it may wrestle you to the ground. Lay or toss the rig into the shallow water where it won't float away.

Now go get your board. You may drag it, if you wish, in soft sand, but you protect it more by carrying it. Turn it on edge with the top surface toward you. Put your near hand in the mast-step slot. Reach over the board with the other hand and grasp the dagger-board trunk. To save an extra trip, you can carry the dagger board over your arm. When you drop the hull into the water, be sure it is deep enough so that the skeg is clear

TOP: Carry the rigging with the boom pointed upwind.
BOTTOM: The lightweight hull should be carried
edgewise against your hip.

of the bottom and won't hit a submerged rock.

If you are new to windsurfing, you might be wise to try your sea legs now, before attaching the sail. Although it is larger, heavier, and more stable than a standard surfboard, a sailboard can be very skittish until you have practiced and acquired proper balance.

So, while the board is afloat in knee-deep water, climb onto it. Center yourself on the board, face forward, and rise to your knees. You will feel top-heavy as you raise your center of gravity, yet you should have little trouble keeping your balance. Now go all the way and stand upright near the mast step. You may wobble a little, perhaps even fall off into the water. But with very little practice you will get the feel of the board.

Now jump back into the water, get your rigged sail, and bring it over to the board. Take the mast foot and push it firmly into the mast-step slot. It must fit tightly enough to stay put in rough water, but you should be able to pluck it out of the socket quickly whenever you want. If the fit is loose, you may need to wrap a little duct or masking tape around the foot to take up the slack. Some mast-foot connections are equipped with adjustable expansion devices that keep them snug in the step yet easy to release.

Since the mast foot includes the universal joint, the

The mast foot should fit snugly into the mast step.

mast and sail simply lie in the water once the mast is stepped. Having checked your other lines to be sure the sail is properly stretched, you turn to the uphaul line, a very important part of your free-sail system. The uphaul line is used primarily to raise the mast and sail out of the water. It is fairly heavy and so is easy to grasp. Often it is linked with a short length of elastic bungee cord or is made with a rubber core to give it stretch.

The upper end of the uphaul attaches to the boom head. Under fairly calm conditions, most windsurfers do not bother to secure the lower end of the uphaul. However, in heavy air or rough water you had better make a habit of anchoring the uphaul to the mast foot so it does not swing or float out of reach when you need it. You can tie a few simple knots along the uphaul's length to aid your grip.

With the mast stepped into the hull and the sail lying downwind in the water, check to be sure that you are in water that is deeper than your dagger board is long. Insert the dagger board down through the well and press it into place. You are now ready to get back aboard and sail off.

Stand beside the floating hull on the upwind side, with your back directly to the wind. Swing the board so that its long axis is at a right angle to the wind. With the sail lying in the water on the far side of the board, the mast will align itself naturally downwind, or leeward, of the hull, which is where you want it to be.

Climb onto the center of the board. If the water is not too deep, you can easily step or jump up onto it. If necessary, you can grasp the far edge of the hull or give a little tug on the uphaul line to help pull yourself up.

Once you are standing upright, position your feet quickly along the center line of the hull, that is, an imaginary line stretching down the middle of the board from bow to stern. Put your front foot forward of the mast and your back foot on or near the dagger-board trunk located directly behind the mast step. Pause now until you have your balance and feel comfortable.

With the sail still lying flat in the water, reach down and take hold of the uphaul. With your back to the wind and knees slightly bent, start pulling the sail out of the water with the uphaul. Start slowly, allowing the water to spill out of the sail. As soon as the sail lightens, straighten your back and pull in quickly on the uphaul. Mast and sail come up easily.

As the clew end of the boom comes out of the water, the leech edge of the sail automatically swings down-

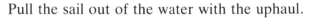

Pull the sail out of the water with the uphaul.

wind like a weather vane and luffs naturally in the breeze. Thus, the sail stands neutral, free of any wind pressure.

While you stand there holding onto the uphaul with both hands, experiment a moment with a few basics. Tilt the mast toward the front of the board, and watch the bow start to swing downwind. Tip the mast back past vertical and toward the stern, and the bow starts to swing up into the wind. Remember: Tilt the mast forward in order to bear off or away from the wind; tip it back to head up into the wind. What you do when you move the mast is shift the focal area of the wind, called the "center of effort" (CE), fore or aft of the dagger board, which resists any sideways motion. If the CE is ahead of the dagger board (mast forward), the bow pivots downwind; if the CE is shifted aft of the dagger board (mast rearward), the bow pivots upwind.

The procedure may sound complicated, but it is simple and logical. As you become more expert, you will find out how to adjust the mast, forward and back, or side to side, in all sorts of subtle ways that change your course. Controlling the tilt of the mast is, in fact, the very foundation of windsurfing.

For now, though, tilt the sail slightly aft while holding onto the uphaul near the mast. As the bow swings slowly upwind, walk right on around the mast with small steps and let the board pivot at the same rate in the opposite direction beneath you. While the sail is hanging slack you can rotate the board around in a full circle. The tilt of the mast and the slight pressure of the wind on the sail will revolve the board, and the force of your moving feet will help also. Bring the mast back to center to stop the rotation. Prepare for the next step.

Stand with the wind at your back and both hands holding the uphaul. The sail luffs downwind and is slack. You want to move forward. Let go of the uphaul with one hand. With that hand, reach over the hand still grasping the uphaul and take hold of the boom fairly close to the mast. Your first hand on the boom, whichever it may be, becomes your mast hand. If sailing to port, your left hand becomes your mast hand; if sailing to starboard, it will be your right hand.

Now, supporting the sail briefly with your mast hand, let go of the uphaul. Drop your free hand to your side for a moment, and twist your body around behind the mast so you look toward the bow. When turning your body, note that your front foot just ahead of the mast pivots naturally to about a forty-five-degree angle forward while your rear foot remains squared off across the dagger-board trunk.

Even as you turn your body, reach with your free

TOP: With sail swinging freely downwind,
take hold of the uphaul with both hands.
BOTTOM: Reach to the forepart of the upwind boom
with one hand.

TOP: Hold the sail upright with the mast hand,
and let go of the uphaul.
BOTTOM: Mast hand and sail hand support the rigging.

hand and grasp the boom in a comfortable position, two feet or so back from the mast. This hand now becomes your sail hand. It will be your right hand when you are sailing to port—that is, whenever the wind fills the left side of your sail—and your left hand when you are sailing to starboard. Always the forward hand is the mast hand, and the sail hand is the one back on the boom.

Everything feels good. You are reasonably sure of your balance. The dagger board, which stabilizes you by resisting roll and side slippage, is down. Your hands are in place on the boom as you hold the mast vertical. Your feet have taken the stance of an Olympic fencer. Now you should sheet in as you practiced on the simulator. You tug on the boom with your sail hand and . . . *kerplop!*

Get used to it. Everyone falls off the board now and then, amateurs and experts alike. Some do so a lot more often than others. All consider a spill part of the fun. As you become more expert the splashes will decrease.

Many things contribute to a ducking: a gust of wind, a sudden moment of calm, the surging wake of a boat that passed unnoticed a minute ago, failing to let go of the boom when you want to regain balance. There are

Sheet in, lean back, and sail off.

an almost infinite number of little things that can upset
your equilibrium and plummet you into the water.

Much of the time you can prevent an upset by letting
go of the boom and reaching for the uphaul line. The
sail quickly spills its air, luffs downwind, and falls into

Sometimes you are wise to drop your sail in the water
and start over again.

the water on the leeward side of the board. With no
sail pressure to contend with, and holding onto the
uphaul with both hands, you should have little diffi-
culty keeping your balance on the board. Then, still
holding the lower end of the uphaul, square the board
sideways to the wind with the pressure of your feet and
begin again.

70

Raise your sail, trying to make your moves flow smoothly into each other without jerking or long pauses. During these few seconds, judge the direction and the force of the wind. Keep your back to it as best you can. Remember, whatever happens to you and your sailboard now depends upon how well or poorly you use the wind.

With the mast upright and your hands positioned properly on the boom, you pull it in slowly with your sail hand. You feel the Dacron triangle harden a bit as

Tilt the mast forward to turn downwind.

it starts to catch the breeze. Straighten your back and lean outward away from the sail, bracing against the wind and pushing your feet strongly against the board.

You sheet in a little harder, and the sail stiffens even more. If a gust starts to topple you, ease off quickly on the boom with your sail hand, spilling air. The bow starts to swing sharply upwind. You tilt the mast forward, and the bow falls off downwind. You hold your course by moving the mast gently. You bring the boom up level, holding it parallel to the surface of the water. The bow hisses over the riffles, leaving a foamy wake behind. You are elated by the sensation of having the wind in your hands. Your speed increases.

You are under way.

chapter six

SETTING YOUR COURSE

You soon learn the basic skills of supporting the mast with your front hand, trimming the sail with your rear hand, and balancing yourself along the board's center line. It becomes second nature to tilt the mast forward so the bow will swing downwind and to pull it toward the stern in order to point upwind. You have taken plenty of spills. But you have always climbed back onto the board and started over. You have sailed around on the smaller ponds. Now the time has come to break out and head toward the bigger bodies of water.

Like all sailing vessels, a sailboard can go upwind, downwind, or crosswind, but it cannot always sail on a direct line to its destination. At times, depending upon the character of the wind and the course you choose, you must break your journey into portions, or legs, and take a zigzag course in order to reach your mark. How efficiently you do so depends upon how carefully

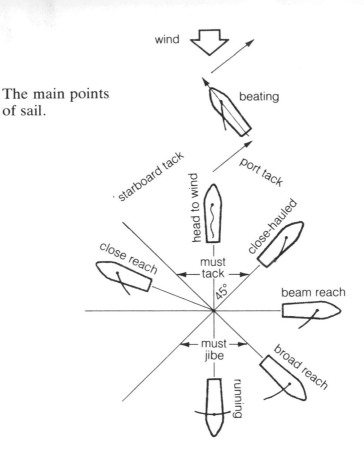

wind

The main points
of sail.

beating

starboard tack

port tack

head to wind

close-hauled

close reach

must
tack

45°

beam reach

must
jibe

broad reach

running

you plan your route and how well you manage your
sail.

There are three general categories of courses: a
beat, sailing steeply upwind; a reach, sailing at an
angle across the wind; and a run, sailing with the wind
directly behind the boat. All are broad terms and
sometimes overlap each other. One sailor's beat may
be another's close reach, and a broad reach may seem
like a run. The designation is of little importance as

long as you are able to keep on your planned course.

In order to arrive at an upwind destination, you must sail at an angle into the wind, or tack. But you are limited by how directly into the wind you can sail. In fact, if you try to steer your craft at much less than an angle of forty-five degrees into the wind, your sharply slanted sail will not take hold. Unable to catch the wind properly, the sail will flap aimlessly from the mast, or luff up. Without propulsion, your sailboard stalls.

But if you set your course at any angle more than forty-five degrees across the wind, you usually can catch enough air to harden your sail and provide

Tacking in a mild breeze involves
sailing at an angle into the wind.

forward thrust. When you run out of sailing room or your angle begins to take you too far away from your destination, you switch direction by coming about (bringing the bow up and through the wind) and tacking off on an opposite angle.

Sometimes you can reach your upwind goal with two long tacks, one to port and one to starboard. Or you may need to beat to windward by zigzagging in a series of short tacks. In either case, tacking, also known as beating, is the way you sail sharply upwind.

Beating upwind is not difficult and provides much windsurfing fun. The prime objective is to sail as close to the wind as you can without luffing up. Assume your normal stance on the board, with your feet along the center line and your back straight, as you lean out against the wind. Pull the boom toward you with your sail hand until you feel the sail harden with the wind. If you don't keep it trimmed in tight enough, your sail loses its aerodynamic shape and you will not make as much headway as you should. If you pull it in too far, you spill the wind from the sail and it luffs up, or goes soft. By glancing at the fullness of the sail and feeling its force travel through you to the board, you can tell when you are trimming it right.

In order to help relieve the strain on your muscles,

High-wind boardsailing puts a real strain
on arms, body, and legs.

try to distribute the pressure as evenly as possible between your hands, arms, body, and legs. Occasionally you should switch your grip on the boom from knuckles up to knuckles down to rest your hands and arms. When your legs and back start to ache, you can move your feet or shift your weight slightly to relieve the soreness somewhat. But, regardless of what you do, you will tire and parts of you will hurt on a long sail in a brisk breeze. Thus, the importance of keeping in good physical shape cannot be overemphasized.

While tacking sharply into the wind, or sailing close-hauled, check the ripples streaming back from the bow of your board. The small waves should look about the same on both sides of the bow if you are on a good heading. Slipping sideways too much or pointing too high into the wind creates dissimilar bow waves. Correct your course accordingly by pulling in or easing off a little on the boom.

The time comes when you must switch directions by changing to the opposite tack. This maneuver is called "coming about," and, in this sense, to tack means to change direction while sailing upwind.

As you slice through the water close-hauled and beating sharply windward, you begin your tack by tipping the mast toward the stern. The bow will then swing even more directly upwind, beyond the effective angle for the sail. The sail spills its air and luffs up. But the momentum of the turn carries the bow right on through the eye of the wind.

While the sail empties, let go of the boom with your back hand. Reach past your mast hand and take hold of the uphaul line. While the sail is still limp, let go of the boom with your mast hand as quickly and smoothly as you can and grip the uphaul line with it also. As you are doing so and as the bow continues to swing past the wind, step around in front of the mast. Take small steps so your movement is a counterbalance to the movement of the board as it changes direction.

The stern swings under the aft boom tip so the sail is set on the opposite side of the board. Your steps bring you halfway around the mast. Now let go of the uphaul with your new mast hand. It will be the opposite hand from the one you used during the previous windward tack.

Grasp the boom with the mast hand, crook your elbow, and pull the mast upright. Position your feet so they are comfortably braced forward, and let go of the uphaul with your sail hand. Reach back along the boom and sheet in to fill the sail. This repositioning sends you skimming off at a right angle to your previous course. Since it is accomplished by using the uphaul rope, the whole procedure for coming about is often called a "rope tack."

There is a faster way to come about, but you need to be fairly expert on your board to use it. You start in much the same way as you do to execute a rope tack, but you don't touch the uphaul. Instead, you tip the mast back sharply until the boom tip bounces off the water. Then pull in quickly with your sail hand, sheeting the sail hard toward you. The combined maneuvers rotate the bow sharply through the wind. As it slackens downwind for a moment, keep both hands on the boom, but slide them together up near the mast. (Some windsurfers grasp the mast itself.) At the same time, step quickly up in front of the mast, facing rearward. Don't get too far forward on the hull, or you may force the bow underwater. With your near hand, reach around the mast and grasp the forepart of the opposite boom. Step on around to the far side of the board. Bring the other hand around beside the first hand. Slide the first hand back to where it now becomes the sail hand. Sheet in, lean back, and slant off on a new tack.

It is important that you practice tacking in both directions—port and starboard—so that your weaker

Step around the mast to come about with a simple tack.

hand becomes used to taking its turn as the sail hand, which requires more strength. In fact, since one arm is not usually as strong as the other, you might be wise to sail extra starboard or port tacks in order to strengthen the weaker muscles.

Going downwind, or running, may seem easier than beating your way to windward. Usually it is, but not always. Running before the wind can be tricky as it calls for a different kind of balance. A stiff breeze or a sudden gust can quickly pull you forward off the board.

Once you are headed generally downwind, tilt the

Proper sail position for running with the wind.

mast forward to bear off still more. Then, with the wind directly at your back, draw the mast up so it is vertical to the board. Next tilt the mast so the tip is well off to one side of the center line, and raise the boom up to a horizontal position on the other side. Now the sail area extends out from the board on both sides. This placement of the sail shifts the center of effort directly over your board and keeps it balanced. Spread your hands on the boom, and stand straddling the dagger board, with one foot a little ahead of the other to brace yourself against any sudden gust that might pull you off balance.

With the wind at your back, you skim along like a sailboat under a balloon spinnaker. Since you are going directly downwind, with no side pressure on your sail, you may lift your dagger board part or all the way out of the trunk to lessen or eliminate the drag it causes in the water. If you remove the dagger board entirely, you will need to carry it by looping the handle over your arm so it is ready to reinsert in the trunk when needed. To adjust your direction, tilt the sail gently to starboard in order to swing the bow to port or to port in order to swing to starboard.

Now that the sail is crossing the board at a right angle in front of your eyes, you make good use of the transparent window sewed into it. Without it, your view ahead would be blocked.

When sailing downwind, you are moving along with the waves, which sometimes gives you the impression of standing still. Yet the chop of the waves tends to make your balance more precarious. With the sail abeam of the hull, your grip on the boom helps steady you fore and aft, but it doesn't help much side to side. If you begin to wobble, reinsert your dagger board or lower your center of gravity by kneeling or squatting.

When you are not beating sharply to windward or running directly downwind, you will be sailing on a reach. A reach is simply sailing with the wind coming at you from the side. If the wind comes directly over the side and you sail at an angle of approximately ninety degrees to it, you are on a beam reach. If the wind hits the boat at a smaller angle, you are on a close reach. If it comes at a larger angle, you are on a broad reach. A reach covers any course except a beat hard to windward or a run directly before the wind.

When sailing on a reach, you adjust the position of your feet, body, and sail hand accordingly. On a beam reach, you sheet in the sail so it lies almost parallel to the hull's center line. In a brisk breeze that is pushing the sail hard to leeward, you must lean far back and spread your feet wide in order to brace yourself and keep your balance. You can improve your grip on the boom by moving your mast hand back about a foot in order to take some of the strain off your sail hand. Also by leaning far back from the boom, you can straighten out your arms, which is a much more relaxing position than bent elbows when trying to control the wind force. The dagger board should be down in order to resist lateral movement, and the skeg helps guide your course. Without them, the sideways pressure of the wind would send you skidding off across the surface, if you did not capsize first.

You sail a close reach very much as you do a beam reach, except that you point higher into the wind. Sheet in the boom a little tighter to keep the wind in your sail. Also lean more toward the stern so your legs push forward, transferring energy from the sail to the board.

A broad reach lies in a generally downwind direction

Sailing a broad reach.

and requires a somewhat different technique. With the wind coming from an angle astern, you tilt your mast forward and to windward, but somewhat less than if you were running directly before the wind. Then you adjust the mast to port or starboard in order to stay on a straight course. Try to keep the boom level. Position both feet behind the mast, since the pull is toward the bow, and brace yourself against it. In effect, you are sailing a downwind tack.

Whatever your tack, the time will come when you need to change it. One way to do so is to jibe. A jibe is used to change direction while sailing downwind. It is an opposite maneuver to coming about into the wind. When jibing, you swing the sail across the bow of the boat instead of across the stern, so the whole procedure changes.

While cruising along on your downwind reach, you ease off on the boom and let the wind fill the sail. Move your front foot up near but not ahead of the mast. Keep your rear foot placed well back on the dagger-board case for balance. Tilt the mast forward so the bow of your board swings directly downwind. Take hold of the uphaul with your mast hand. At about the same time, let go of the boom with your sail hand and transfer this hand to the uphaul. Move your feet so you straddle the dagger-board trunk.

Holding onto the uphaul with both hands, let the wind carry the sail across the bow so it points to leeward. You can help the rotation a little with a

Jibe by swinging the sail downwind across the bow, and reach for the opposite boom.

rhythmic tug on the uphaul. As the opposite boom swings into view, reach for it with your new sail hand. Set your feet in normal stance, one by the mast and one back near the dagger board. Release the uphaul and tug the mast upright with your front hand. Now you are in position to sheet in the sail and take off on your new downwind heading.

This maneuver can be thought of as a rope jibe, similar but opposite to the earlier-described rope tack. Again some surfers bypass the uphaul rope and prefer simply to grab hold of the mast or front bumper as they pivot through the jibe. The details are less important than doing what comes naturally and what works best for you.

However, to windsurf with style and with skill, you should first master the basics of tacking into the wind and reaching across or downwind. You also must practice your turns, both into and away from the wind, for the real test of a windsurfer is being able to alter your course as quickly and effortlessly as possible. When you have reached this stage and have become one with your board and sail, you are ready for stronger winds, rougher water, and the excitement of competition.

chapter seven
RACING

One way to add to the fun of windsurfing is to share it with others. Joining a group of boardsailors will undoubtedly enhance your enjoyment of the sport and also provide further safety. Participation in group activities is a good way to learn new techniques, and as you improve you can make your own contributions.

Windsurfing groups are usually easy to locate. They can be found almost anyplace in the United States, Canada, Australia, Asia, or Europe. Probably your local sailboard dealer can tip you off to a nearby fleet that is looking for new members. A fleet can number from half a dozen windsurfing sailors to several hundred or so. As a member of a fleet you help plan activities and events that provide the most fun while you also become increasingly competent on your board.

You will find that once you have mastered such basics as balance, steering, and sail management, your confidence and windsurfing skills improve amazingly fast. Soon you will want to try stronger winds and heavier surfs and pit your sailing talents against others.

After all, you have read about the fellow who windsurfed around Cape Horn, an area known the world over for its furious winds and rough water. There also was the young French adventurer who, in the autumn of 1979, started from Alaska and boardsailed across the frigid, turbulent waters of the Bering Strait all the way to Russian Siberia. And a host of windsurfers regularly sail across the broad expanse of ocean that separates the individual islands of the Hawaiian chain. You begin to feel that you are ready to take on the world with your sailboard.

Take your time, however. First, develop your skills in well-planned stages. Spend at least a couple of dozen sailing hours on moderately calm water in winds that do not exceed a velocity of Force 4.

When you fall less frequently, when your feet feel at home on the board, when trimming your sail in tricky winds becomes second nature, try sailing in a Force-5 wind of perhaps nineteen or twenty knots. Keeping your board flat on the water as the wind tries to tip you over or tear the sail from your hands will not be easy. If you allow the board to heel over too much while

Forceful winds test a windsailor's mettle.

sheeting in against the wind, the tilted dagger board cutting upward through the water begins to act like a wing. It may lift to the surface and tip you over without warning. Or, while you are leaning far back with your shoulders almost touching the water as you hold the boom with aching arms, you may hit an unseen pocket of quiet air. Caught suddenly in the lull, the sail loses wind pressure and slackens, and in you go! Don't be discouraged. Even the experts get dunked.

So, by all means, try the ever-stronger winds. Tackle them from every quarter. Beat into them with zigzagging tacks to port and to starboard. Take them on with slanting reaches from both sides so that right and left hands and arms take turns at the mast and sail and become equally strong and adept.

Keep in mind the temperature of both wind and water. Be cautious if you start shivering involuntarily whether in or out of the water. The exposure can bring on dangerous hypothermia. Wear your wet suit or at least some kind of shirt, sweater, or pants to protect you from the wind and help keep the body heat in.

Rough water produces unique windsurfing problems. To a point, your board is long enough and stable enough to ride over or through a choppy surface and be unaffected by minor tides or currents. But large bodies of water often generate waves and currents that will test your skills to the utmost.

Reasonably small waves or rolling swells, say a foot or two high, should not bother you. When sailing upwind into one, simply shift your weight a bit toward

White water produces unique windsurfing problems.

your rear foot to bring the bow up. Turn toward the swell and ride over it at a fairly sharp angle to keep from being upset by the surge. Going into a wave on a shallow slant can capsize you and perhaps damage your mast and sail as it rolls you over. On the far side of the swell, shift your weight forward to bring the bow down into the trough to keep headway. Small waves usually add to the fun of even the inexperienced windsurfer.

Be careful, however, if you should do some long-distance sailboarding. You may venture unwittingly then into strange waters with tides surging through a narrow strait or strong currents swirling around a point of land. Without a favorable wind, you might find yourself in the dangerous situation of being carried out to sea or swept toward the rocks.

Although most windsurfers start by seeking recreational pleasure from the sport, sooner or later you probably will feel the urge to compete. Windsurfing is the kind of outdoor activity that lends itself to matching one's skills against those of others, and there are plenty of opportunities to do so.

For instance, you can participate in a long-distance race from one point to another. You can run a zigzag slalom course similar to a skier's. Or you can race over a measured triangular course similar to the type used by small-boat sailors. Boards with the lightest weight are the fastest and have a competitive advantage. So if a large number enter an event, the regatta is then divided into lightweight, middleweight, and heavyweight classes in order to equalize the competition.

The triangle race rapidly gained popularity when boardsailing was approved by the International Olympic Committee (IOC) as an added event in the 1984 Olympics. In effect, sailboards qualified as an official small boat class. Today, whether or not you aspire to

Leisurely windsurfing can even include passenger service.

the Olympics, you will find many sailboard races being run over Olympic-style courses.

The Olympic course is laid out in the shape of a triangle, having three equal sides. The corner angles are each sixty degrees. The first leg of the course is laid directly upwind. At the starting signal, you beat your way windward by using a series of zigzagging tacks. Usually racing in a counterclockwise direction, you round the first, or windward, mark and slant off downwind on a broad reach toward the second, or reaching, mark. At the reaching mark, you jibe and set off on an opposite reach toward the third, or leeward, mark. Rounding it, you turn back into the wind, slip your dagger board into place—since you probably removed it when you were sailing the reach—and repeat the first leg.

The Olympic racing course.

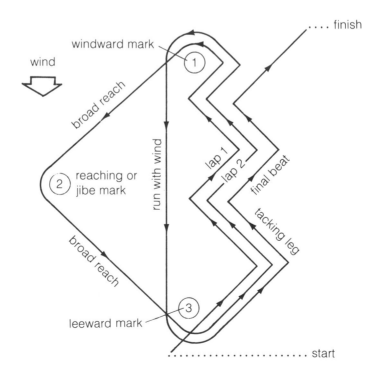

In heavy air, a back-supporting harness
eases the strain of handling the boom.

By now your arms and legs ache with the pressure.
Fortunately, you have equipped yourself with a harness designed to relieve the strain. The harness is a
webbed nylon vest or special padded, lightweight
jacket with a quick-release hook strapped in front. The
other essential parts of the harness assembly are rope
loops attached strategically to each side of the wishbone boom. Both the harness and rope loops are
readily adjustable.

When the wind bulges the sail, threatening to tear
the boom from your tiring hands, you hook in by
sliding the harness hook onto the rope loop. Then you

lean back and let the harness support your weight. It takes most of the pressure off your hands and arms. Now you can use them to make the constant delicate sail adjustments needed without having to fight the wind.

Having beaten your way back to the windward mark for the second time, you tack around it once more. But now, instead of going out on another reach, you make a 180-degree turn, raise your dagger board again, and run directly downwind back to the leeward mark. After rounding it for the second time, you make a final beat upwind to the finish line. A strenuous race, it is designed to test the three basic sailing techniques of beating, reaching, and running.

Although the Olympic-style course is generally favored, changes in racing layouts often are made at different regattas to best fit the geography, wind conditions, or other unique factors of an area. However, regardless of the course over which you compete, you are certain to find that racing provides both fun and a worthy test of your windsurfing skills.

You may also want to try slalom racing, which takes place over a buoy-marked course. The floats may be beach balls, empty plastic jugs, or any highly visible objects that can be anchored in place. The slalom

A flock of racers jockey for position
as they head toward a mark.

course can be laid out in a variety of patterns—straight line, rectangular, or whatever will test your ability to execute various sailing maneuvers.

Sometimes the slalom is run with two racers starting off in opposite directions around the course and meeting head on somewhere along the route. Or a race may be made up of several laps, going clockwise, counterclockwise, or in a weaving pattern around the buoys. Some slaloms are of a pursuit type, in which the

Officials aboard a committee boat monitor a race.

racers start ten or fifteen seconds behind each other and try to overtake and pass as many opponents as possible in the shortest amount of time.

Slalom racing provides a great deal of close-quarter, rapid-fire action. The strenuous maneuvering and attempts to outwit your opponent are extremely demanding. Usually the winner is the sailor who concentrates the most and performs the fastest, smoothest turns.

Long-distance racing is an event that also will tax you to the fullest. It can cover any distance, although six miles (approximately ten kilometers) is the average. The course may be a triangle, similar to the Olympic course, or it may be laid out in other ways.

Ideally, it should be planned so it tests your skills in upwind, downwind, and crosswind tactics.

Since the distance on each leg is quite long, the strain on your body is increasingly great. More than ever you need to use a trapeze harness to help support your weight and preserve your strength. Still, the combination of shifting winds and tiring limbs may cause you to lose control and take a ducking every now and then. In high winds, few escape. But the one who stays dry the longest usually ends up at or near the front of the pack.

Long-distance racing is so demanding that it requires some special equipment. For instance, since falls are commonplace and may occur far from land, you should use some kind of tether that will hold your sail rig and the board together in case of a spill. The sail will remain pretty much where it falls in the water, but the lightweight board may be carried away by the wind. If you don't have a tether, you should be sure to stay with the board when everything is down. It is buoyant and, therefore, your best life preserver.

Although you probably are not one to give up easily, there are times in a race or even in a leisurely sail when the wind acts up, you take frequent spills, and you get too cold. Every time you climb back up onto the board

Being towed in.

and raise the sail the effort takes something out of you. When you are upright, the strong, gusting winds become harder to handle. Now is the time to practice prudence and save yourself for another try at another time. Get to shore.

A fellow windsurfer may detect that you're in trouble and come over to give you a hand. He or she may offer to tow you back to the beach, which is fairly easy when done properly.

If you are still in the water, get busy and untie the knots holding your boom at the mast and clew. Lay the

boom on your sailboard. If it hasn't already popped
out, pull the mast foot out of the step. Gather in the
sail. Better still, roll it around the mast and wrap a line
around it. Pull out your dagger board and lay it on the
hull by the boom. Now place the mast and rolled-up
sail lengthwise atop the board. Hoist yourself up and
lie beside it.

As your rescuer approaches from windward, ease up
to the lee side of his board. Take hold of the strap on
his dagger board, or grip whatever else is handy, and
accept a tow home.

If there is no one around to aid you, go through the
same procedure—dismantle your rig, roll up your sail,
and stack everything on the board. Then, lying prone
atop the hull, start hand paddling your way in as any

The self-rescue system is simple and safe.

surfboarder would do. If that effort becomes too tiring, sit on the hull and use your dagger board for a paddle. This self-rescue system works nicely, so there is never a cause for panic.

Plenty of little nagging problems turn up in windsurfing competitions, such as broken lines, a torn sail, a cracked dagger board, or a dented hull. But the real emergencies are few and far between. So go out and share in the fun.

chapter eight
FREESTYLE STUNTS

As in many sports, the time comes when you can't resist the urge to pull out all the stops, kick up your heels, and cut fancy capers. Some people say you are hot dogging. Those who don't understand may say you are showing off. Officially your stunts are called "freestyle." That term is an apt description, for it indicates freedom of movement and stylish action. The idea of freestyle windsurfing is to perform the most daring, difficult, and bizarre maneuvers you can with your board. You do them for your own satisifaction as well as for the wide-eyed amazement of anyone who might be watching from the shore.

Of course, before attempting the difficulties of freestyle windsurfing, you must master the basics of how best to use the four elements with which you work—wind, water, board, and sail. Even so, you can expect to take a good many unscheduled dunkings.

There is a long list of well-tested freestyle tricks to

work with. The list grows ever longer as imaginative and inventive windsurfers create new moves and test them out in the water. If successful, the trick is sometimes named after the originator.

When you decide to take up freestyling, you should start with some of the more familiar tricks that you have seen others perform. One of the first you might try is the head dip.

While tacking on a fairly stiff Force-4 breeze of about fourteen knots and keeping the wind hard in your sail, arch your back and lean out away from the boom. Then pull yourself back up to the boom. If all goes well, try it again. Only lean out farther this time, and tip your head back. Try to keep your sail in view, and be alert to the boom pressure in your hands. If you sheet in too much, you will luff the sail, lose wind support, and flop backward into the water. But if you flex your legs, body, and neck to the fullest and keep good wind in the sail to support your outward weight, you should be able to dip the top of your head in the water. You can even drag it along a few feet before hoisting yourself back upright.

A similar but more difficult maneuver done in reverse is the face dip. For it, you turn your back to the sail and grip the boom with arms extended behind you. To execute the stunt, you must coordinate your mind and muscles so that you trim the boom with the reverse hand. Once you have adjusted properly to the sail pressure and can manage it in a reverse-hand position, you lean far forward until your nose traces a path in the water. Then try to get yourself straightened back up before a slight lull or change in the wind sends you somersaulting overboard.

After trying the face dip, you might step around to the lee side of the board. It is the wrong side to sail from, but don't give the filled sail a chance to push you off the board. Instead of pulling on the boom in the usual fashion to sheet in the sail, push your weight against the mast and boom. With a little practice, you can steer nicely from the lee side of the board while leaning forward against the mast and boom.

With a little more practice, you should be able to turn around and press your back against the bulging sail. With or without one arm extended out on the boom, you can skim along casually with your back to the rigging.

For an added bit of effect, you can even slip inside the boom, with your back still to the sail. As you can see, the very essence of freestyle windsurfing is to keep adding variety to a trick until you have stretched it to the limits of possibility.

You will enjoy trying several types of pirouettes.

TOP: Riding with back to the sail is
one of the simpler freestyle tricks.
BOTTOM: Sailing from the lee requires
leaning into the wind.

Basically, a pirouette consists of setting up your board and sail so you can let go with both hands for a moment or two without losing control. Once you've released your hold you whirl yourself around a full 360-degree circle and grab the boom again before you lose your balance and go over the side.

There are variations to such whirling-dervish antics. One involves rotating the sail a full 360 degrees around the board. While sailing across a fairly mild wind, swing the clew over the bow of your boat and downwind. Hold the boom steady and walk quickly around the mast, pushing on through the eye of the wind and back to your original position. Generally this stunt is known as a sail 360, or helicopter.

A freestyler abandons the boom for a moment as he swings the sail by its foot.

You can also try a hull 360. Again, while sailing across the wind, rake your mast back toward the stern. As you know from earliest training, this adjustment swings the bow up into the wind. Keep the sail stationary and take small steps to help turn the board a full rotation under your feet.

You might want to test out some tricky tacks too. Until now you have come about by swinging the bow up into and through the wind while stepping around in front of the mast and taking hold of the opposite boom. Instead, try this tack as you sail close-hauled into the wind. Sheet in still more, and when you feel the sail soften just before it luffs up, tip the mast sharply and directly upwind. Now the clew is tilted high into the air. Step around behind the mast, duck under the sail, reach for the opposite boom, and bear off on a new heading. This maneuver is the duck tack.

If you want to dress up the old tried-and-true way of coming about, you can try the spin tack. As you step around in front of the mast, let go of it just long enough to switch hands as you do a spinning pirouette around the mast and take up your position on the opposite side of the board.

Some of the most spectacular freestyle tricks come under the heading of railrides—the rail being the edge of the board. You need a brisk wind in which to perform proper railrides and give them drama. When conditions are right, start your railride by sailing on a beam reach with hands and feet in normal position on boom and board. While skimming along, slip your back foot across the center line in order to shift weight toward the lee side of the hull. This position tilts the windward edge slightly up out of the water. Quickly hook your front foot under that edge and, still holding the mast and sail upright, flip the board onto its rail so it stands edgewise in the water.

While the shin of your forward leg kneels uncomfortably on the narrow rim for a moment, bring your other foot up and raise yourself to a standing position on the rail. Keep the mast tilted right up against the top edge of the board. And be sure the mast foot is tight in the slot so it won't slip out during your railride.

From this basic railride, you can develop several fancy variations. You can sit astride the rail and dangle your feet in the water. You can kneel. You can keep one foot on the rail and the other on the protruding dagger board. You can rock the board vigorously fore and aft while riding it edgewise through the water.

The freestyle tricks you are able to display on a sailboard are as wide and varied as your imagination,

From a basic railride (above), you can develop
several fancy variations:
You can ride inside the boom (below),
or with one foot on the dagger board (opposite, top),
or even do a railride wheelie (opposite, bottom).

Try sailing the board upside down.

creativity, and, of course, ability will allow. You can sail upside down on the board and manage the boom with your feet. You may even team up with some lightweight, nimble member of your group and do shoulder carries or other gymnastic tricks while keeping the sailboard upright and on its course.

Another way of doubling up on your fun is to sail tandem, or two to a board. The second person is not just a passenger, which is sometimes done. Instead, two windsurfers work separate masts and sails on a specially designed tandem board.

A tandem sailboard is an oversized hull with two mast steps for two sails, one considerably forward of center and one aft. This arrangement, of course, radically changes the steering and stability of the board. You and your sailing partner can count on taking a few falls before you become sufficiently skilled to keep the tandem board from careering wildly across the water. If one sailor fails to harmonize his or her moves with the other, an upset is in the making. One sail tends to deflect or blank out the wind from the other, resulting in a loss of balance. You find that you frequently have to modify the normal rules for tacking, jibing, luffing up, and most other maneuvers, for they work differently on a multimasted sailboard. But figuring out the necessary adjustments is part of the

Sailing a tandem board requires skillful teamwork, but can be lots of fun.

fun, so any time you have a chance to share a tandem sailboard, don't turn it down.

You approach the summit of freestyle sailboarding when the surf is up and the winds are strong. Under such conditions, you can choose to ride the waves shoreward in much the same manner as the familiar surfboarder. There is a major difference, however, for you have not only the board but a sail to think about. It can be both a blessing and a hazard. Instead of paddling with your hands as a surfer does, you use the power of the sail to catch a surging swell and send you planing down its advancing side.

The wind becomes a very critical factor, and you must be expert at handling it. You must check its direction and velocity and make it work for you. Sometimes you use it to steer your board on a slanting course down a wave. Or you may bear off and go straight in with the wave. In any case, you must practice caution. If you get moving fast, there is the chance that you will catch up with the wind. Then your sail will go limp and become useless for steering. Worse, riding the wave may increase your momentum

Riding the surf is a fun-filled challenge,
since you have not only a board but a sail to handle.

until it exceeds the wind speed. The result may be a backwind in your sail, which surely will throw you off balance and probably into the water. You must try to avoid this problem, for with your sail down in a rolling surf, you are apt to end up with a broken mast, a cracked hull, or other damage.

So judge the wind properly and keep plenty of air in your sail. Choose a course to suit the conditions. Then start your traverse across the advancing surf. If you can keep enough wind in your sail to provide positive steering control, bear off and ride it straight in as far as you can. Just be sure to pull out in plenty of time to prevent your dagger board or skeg from crunching in the shallows.

Obviously you should begin your surf riding on small waves, say around two or three feet high. Graduate upward only as is warranted by your improving skills. Someday you may tackle the roaring rollers of Hawaii. When done sensibly, wave surfing becomes one of the most exhilarating windsurfing feats.

The ultimate in windsurfing excitement, however, is wave jumping. It also is an event that demands caution. Again, start small. While windsurfing across a lake, you may be passed by a powerboat. Watch its bow wave roll toward you. Build up what speed you can with your board. Then, just as the small wave arrives, turn into it, shift your weight toward your back foot, bring up the bow, and catapult over the top. You may be airborne for only a few inches, but your jump will make you feel as though you are flying.

After you have teethed your talents on ever-larger waves, the time arrives when you feel you are ready to take off and fly your board. You may need to scout around for a special, high-performance board that is smaller, more scooped at the bow, and equipped with a raked-back racing dagger board and additional skegs to aid stability. You probably will need a storm sail which is smaller than the standard sail and designed for the high winds that usually accompany large waves.

Also, for jumping big waves, you will need to put some foot straps on your board. They are soft loops placed strategically on the aft deck of the hull. By slipping your feet into the straps you can control the board and keep it from falling away when you become airborne. In addition, the straps will help you keep your feet on the board during your landing, which is bound to be rough. You must be sure, however, that your foot straps are roomy enough so you can release your feet from them whenever you want.

Once you are clear of the beach and have set your

Foot straps are needed for wave jumping.

sail to catch a quartering onshore wind, you start your board skimming along on a close reach toward the incoming surf. You watch the nearest wave grow in size, and you race toward it at an angle away from its marching curl. You must get to the wave before it breaks and swamps you in a maelstrom of white water.

You glance down at the foot straps. There are more straps than you have feet. Deciding quickly which pair will provide you the best control over the board, you slip your feet into them.

The rolling wave suddenly seems to tower above you, and the toppling line of the break comes roaring in from the side like a moving waterfall. You seem to be racing right for it. But, just before reaching the break, you sheet in, tilt the mast aft, head up into the wind and straight at the wave. Under full, sail-snapping speed, with spray peppering your face, you thrust your board straight at the wave. The bow leaps sharply upward as it climbs the steep wall of surging water.

Then, like a missile, you take off from the crest. You are fully airborne, flying. You fight to hold the board level so that you neither flip over backward nor nose-dive into the trough. You are not sure just how far you fly through the air. Maybe you go ten feet, perhaps thirty. You brace for the landing. Having gone this far, you are reasonably sure that you can keep board and sail under control. In fact, you glance ahead toward the next oncoming wave.

You delight in the whole challenging adventure. You have learned your skills well. You have enjoyed leisurely boardsailing with friends. You have cruised on mild zephyrs, raced in regattas, ridden the surf, jumped waves, and, indeed, cavorted freestyle wherever you could find water to sail on. You have tasted

real excitement, relished adventure, experienced the
thrill of competition and the pride of achievement.

But, most of all, your greatest prize is the fun you
get when the wind is at your back, filling your sail.

Wave jumping is boardsailing at its exhilarating best.

glossary

abeam—directly from the side, at right angles to the board.

aft—toward the stern, or back, of a boat.

airfoil shape—the sail's winglike configuration.

apparent wind—the adjusted wind direction caused by the board's forward speed.

batten—the stiffening slat inserted along the sail leech.

beam reach—to sail directly across, or at a ninety-degree angle to, the wind.

bear off—to turn downwind (opposite of *luff up* or *head up*).

beat—to sail upwind; to weather.

boom—the spar used to stretch out the bottom of the sail; also used to control the sailboard's rig.

bow—the most forward part of a sailing vessel.

broad reach—to sail on a course angling moderately downwind.

center of effort (CE)—a constantly changing focal point through which aerodynamic wind forces act on the sail.

clew—the rear corner of the sail farthest from the mast.

close-hauled—to sail as steeply upwind as possible; on the wind.

close reach—to sail a course somewhat upwind of a beam reach.

come about—to change direction by bringing the bow up and through the wind; to tack.

crosswind—a wind that blows across the direction of travel.

Dacron—DuPont-trademarked polyester fiber sailcloth often favored by wind sailors.

dagger board—a movable, keellike centerboard lowered through the sailboard hull to prevent sideways drift.

downhaul—the line that ties the sail tack to the mast foot.

downwind—with the wind.

fore—toward the front end, or bow, of the boat.

freestyle—innovative windsurfing tricks.

harness—a trapezelike sailing aid that hooks up to the boom and is used by a wind sailor to ease the strain on body and limbs.

heading—the point on the compass or horizon toward which to sail.

head up—to turn upwind (opposite of *bear off*).

hull—the frame or body of a ship exclusive of rigging, mast, and sail; the board.

hypothermia—a dangerous reduction in body temperature due to excessive exposure to cold.

inhaul—the line that ties the boom to the mast.

jibe—to alter course while turning downwind (opposite to *tack*).

knot—a nautical mile (about 6060 feet) per hour.

leech—the back edge of the sail between the head and the clew.

leeward—the side away from the wind (opposite to *windward*).

luff—a) the forward edge of the sail; b) to have the sail flap loosely when not wind filled.

luff up—to turn into the wind (opposite of *bear off*).

mark—a floating buoy or other object marking a race course.

mast—a vertical spar that supports the sail.

mast foot—the lower end of the mast.

mast hand—the boom hand nearest the mast.

mast head—the top of the mast.

mast step—a socket into which the mast foot fits.

Mylar—a waterproof plastic sail material.

offshore wind—the wind blowing from land toward water.

onshore wind—the wind blowing from water toward land.

on the wind—to sail as nearly against the wind as possible; close-hauled.

124

outhaul—the line that stretches the sail clew toward the boom end.

pearl—to have the bow of the hull nose underwater.

port—the side of a vessel to the left when facing forward.

port tack—to sail with the wind coming from the left side.

rake—to lean the mast and sail in any direction.

reach—to sail across the wind.

rig—the mast, sail, and boom assembly.

rocker—a slight upward bend to the sailboard stern.

run—to sail directly downwind.

sail hand—the hand aft, or rearward, on the boom.

scoop—an upward bend in the bow of the hull.

sheet in—to pull on the boom with the sail hand to catch the wind.

sheet out—to ease off on the boom to spill wind.

skeg—a small, stabilizing fin set beneath the stern of the hull.

starboard—the side of a vessel to the right when facing forward.

starboard tack—to sail with the wind coming from the right side.

stern—the after end of a sailing vessel; to the rear.

tack—a) the lower front corner of the sail; b) to sail at an angle to the wind; c) to come about upwind (opposite to *jibe*).

trim sail—to sheet in or sheet out in order to fine tune the sail.

universal—a freely pivoting base allowing the mast to tip or rotate in any direction.

uphaul—the heavy line used primarily to raise the mast and sail out of the water.

upwind—against the wind.

weather—to windward; to sail upwind.

wet suit—waterproof clothing to insulate against cold and exposure.

windward—the side from which the wind is coming; (opposite to *leeward*).

index

*indicates illustrations